Alister McGrath, a former atheist, is Andreas Idreos Professor of Science and Religion at the University of Oxford. He is one of the leading critics of the 'New Atheism' and regularly comments on its themes. His many books include the international bestseller *The Dawkins Delusion?*, cowritten with Joanna Collicutt McGrath.

Little Books of Guidance
Finding answers to life's big questions!

Also in the series:

WHY ARE WE HERE?

A little book of guidance

ALISTER McGRATH

First published in Great Britain in 2015

Society for Promoting Christian Knowledge
36 Causton Street
London SW1P 4ST
www.spck.org.uk

British Library Cataloguing-in-Publication Data
A catalogue record for this book is available from the British Library

ISBN 978–0–281–07438–9
eBook ISBN 978–0–281–07442–6

Typeset by Graphicraft Limited, Hong Kong
First printed in Great Britain by Ashford Colour Press
Subsequently digitally printed in Great Britain

eBook by Graphicraft Limited, Hong Kong

Produced on paper from sustainable forests

Contents

1

Beyond the scientific horizon

In 1885, Thomas H. Huxley, the great champion of Charles Darwin's ideas in Victorian England, delivered a speech to mark the completion of a statue of Darwin, which would soon grace a London museum. In drawing the speech to a close, Huxley declares that science 'commits suicide when it adopts a creed'.[1] It is one of his most perceptive statements, and it deserves close attention.

Huxley is not simply noting the dangers which arise when science becomes the servant of the church or of any religious organization or theological orthodoxy. He sees equal danger in science's becoming the servant of a doctrinaire atheism, or being seen as a weapon in a war against religious belief. Science, he argues, is *science*, not a tool in the hands of those with aggressive religious or manipulative anti-religious agendas. Though often portrayed as a critic of religion, Huxley's main concern is to ensure that science is free to conduct its pursuit of truth without interference from dogmatism of any kind – whether religious or anti-religious.[2]

Science, when at its best and most authentic, has no creed, whether religious or anti-religious. As Huxley himself points out, it nevertheless has one, and only one, article of faith:

> The one act of faith in the convert to science, is the con-
> fession of the universality of order and of the absolute
> validity in all times and under all circumstances, of the law
> of causation. This confession is an act of faith, because, by
> the nature of the case, the truth of such propositions is not
> susceptible of proof.[3]

While there are those who insist that science makes
and requires no judgement of faith, this is clearly not
the case, in Huxley's view. Science finds itself dependent
upon certain working beliefs which are not 'susceptible
of proof', which Huxley rightly terms 'acts of faith'. For
obvious reasons, New Atheist writers have been reluctant
to draw attention to Huxley's insight, which contrasts
sharply with the dogmatic insistence of Richard Dawkins
that science is a faith-free zone. Dawkins is out of line with
the philosophy of science here. Science has to make some
basic assumptions – the sort of thing that the psychologist
William James helpfully terms 'working hypotheses'.

The astonishing, almost pathological aversion of the
New Atheism to faith-based judgements in science ultimately seems to reflect little more than a prejudice against
religion and its vocabulary. The philosopher of science
Michael Polanyi is one of many writers to emphasize
the fundamental importance of the scientific belief in the
rationality of the natural world, along with an expectation
that this will continue to manifest itself in the empirical
investigation of the world.

Yet is science by itself capable of satisfying the human
quest for meaning? One of the most perceptive dis-
cussions of this question comes from the pen of the
Spanish philosopher José Ortega y Gasset (1883–1955),
who celebrates science's capacity to explain our observa-
tions of the world, while nevertheless insisting on its
failure to satisfy the deeper longings and questions of
humanity.

'Scientific truth is characterized by its exactness and the certainty of its predictions. But these admirable qualities are contrived by science at the cost of remaining on a plane of secondary problems, leaving intact the ultimate and decisive questions.'[4]

The fundamental virtue of science is that it knows when to stop. It only answers questions that it knows it can answer on the basis of the evidence. But human curiosity wants to go further than this. Human beings are unable 'to do without all-around knowledge of the world, without an integral idea of the universe. Crude or refined, with our consent or without it, such a trans-scientific picture of the world will settle in the mind of each of us, ruling our lives more effectively than scientific truth.'

Ortega y Gasset declares that the twentieth century witnessed unparalleled efforts to restrain humanity within the realm of the exact and determinable. A whole series of questions are needlessly and improperly declared to be 'meaningless', because they go beyond the limits of the natural sciences. Ortega y Gasset declares that this premature dismissal extends to the great questions of life, such as 'Where does the world come from, and whither is it going? Which is the supreme power of the cosmos, what the essential meaning of life?'

However, we continue to wrestle with such ultimate questions of life, ignoring the demands of those who insist that they are meaningless. We cannot evade these questions, because wrestling with them is an inalienable aspect of being human. 'We are given no escape from ultimate questions. In one way or another they are in us, whether we like it or not. Scientific truth is exact, but it is incomplete.'

To be human is to yearn for meaning and answers to the riddles of existence. Yet the scientific enterprise stops short of those ultimate questions, and rightly so. It knows its limits, and its limits are determined by evidence. But sometimes that evidence seems to point beyond itself, to another world just over the horizon, beyond scientific investigation. Ortega y Gasset uses an illuminating image in making this point.

> Science is but a small part of the human mind and organism. Where it stops, man does not stop. If the physicist detains, at the point where his method ends, the hand with which he delineates the facts, the human being behind each physicist prolongs the line thus begun and carries it on to its termination, as an eye beholding an arch in ruins will of itself complete the missing airy curve.

Ortega y Gasset's evocative image of the ruined arch enables us to grasp an important point. We are not talking about a blind leap of faith in the dark, but the continuation of an intellectual trajectory beyond the thresholds of the scientific method. Faith may go beyond reason and evidence; it does not go against them, but continues their lines of thought.

Thus it is perfectly reasonable to ask whether deeper assumptions about the nature of reality – including the existence and nature and God – are embedded within the scientific method. Science makes no such explicit assumptions. But are such assumptions implicit? Does the scientific enterprise itself point to something which lies beyond its scope to investigate, yet upon which its successes ultimately depend?

The theoretical chemist Charles A. Coulson, for example, points out the importance of religious convictions in explaining the 'unprovable assumption that there is an order and constancy in Nature'.[5] The British philosopher of religion Richard Swinburne takes this further, arguing that the explanatory capacity of faith in God is not limited to the fine details of reality, but extends beyond these to include the great questions of life that are either 'too big' or 'too odd' for science to explain.[6]

It is quite clear that many of the deepest and most engaging questions about the nature of the universe have their origins in a fundamentally religious quest for meaning. The concept of a lawful universe, with order that can be understood and trusted, emerged largely out of fundamental beliefs about the nature of God, expressed in the notion of the 'laws of nature'. Scientific advance has disclosed the fundamental explicability of much of the natural world. Though some might see this as eliminating any notion of mystery, others have rightly pointed out that it raises a far deeper question: why can we explain things at all? Scientists are so used to being able to make sense of the world that they take it for granted.[7] Yet this is actually a rather curious phenomenon.

As Albert Einstein pointed out in 1936, 'The eternal mystery of the world is its comprehensibility.'[8] The fact that the world 'is comprehensible is a miracle'. For Einstein, explicability itself clearly requires explanation. The most incomprehensible thing about the universe is that it is comprehensible. The intelligibility of the natural world, demonstrated by the natural sciences, raises the fundamental question as to why there is such a fundamental resonance between the human mind and the structures of the universe.

Here we see a general pattern: science raises questions which transcend its capacity to answer them. So where do we look for those answers? All guides have their limits. Science is a good guide to truth, which falters when we yearn for meaning. If there is meaning within the world, science is simply not going to be able to disclose it. This is not a criticism of science. It is simply a plea to avoid discrediting science by making it say things that it can't defend by its own methods – such as whether there is a God.

So what of God? As the noted biologist Stephen Jay Gould and countless others have insisted, the question of the existence and nature of God lies beyond the scientific method.[9] Yet some aggressive atheists have tried to argue that science explains (or has the potential to explain) everything, including matters traditionally regarded as lying within the religious realm. The traditional scientific positivist outlook that seems so characteristic of the New Atheism holds that science and religion offer competing explanations. One day science will triumph, and religious explanations will fade away. There cannot be multiple explanations of the same things, and only the scientific explanation can be valid, claims the New Atheism.

Yet this is actually a very nineteenth-century way of arguing, resting on a failure to think critically about the nature of scientific explanation. Neuroscientist Max Bennett and philosopher Peter Hacker have recently explored the science-explains-everything outlook that Dawkins and others espouse: they have found it seriously wanting.[10] For example, scientific theories cannot be said to 'explain the world' – only to explain the *phenomena* which are observed within the world. Furthermore, Bennett and Hacker argue, scientific theories do not, and are not intended to, describe and explain 'everything about the world', such as its purpose. Law, economics and sociology are examples of disciplines which engage with domain-specific phenomena, without in any way having to regard themselves as somehow being inferior to the natural sciences or dependent upon them.

The real issue has to do with levels of explanation. We live in a complex, multi-layered universe. Each level has to be included in our analysis. Physics, chemistry, biology and psychology – to note only four sciences – engage with different levels of reality and offer explanations appropriate to that level. But they are not individually exhaustive. A comprehensive explanation must bring together these different levels of explanation, in that (to give an obvious example) the physical explanation of an electron is not in competition with its chemical counterpart.

My Oxford colleague John Lennox, who is a mathematician and philosopher of science, uses a neat illustration to make this point. Imagine a cake being subjected to scientific analysis, leading to an exhaustive discussion of its chemical composition and of the physical forces which hold it together. Does this tell us that the cake was baked to celebrate a birthday? And is this inconsistent with the scientific analysis? Of course not. Science and theology ask different questions: in the case of science, the question concerns how things happen: by what process? In the case of theology, the question is why things happen: to what purpose?

Here we see the important scientific principle of different levels of explanation, which supplement each other. This principle can easily be explored from everyday life. Consider a performance of your favourite piece of music. This can be scientifically described in terms of patterns of vibrations.

Yet this perfectly valid explanation requires supplementation if it is to account for the full significance of the phenomenon of music and its impact upon us. Similarly, there is far more to a great painting than an analysis of its chemical components or the physical arrangement of its elements.

Scientific and religious explanations can thus supplement each other. The problems start when scientists start pretending to be religious or theologians start pretending to be scientists. Science tells us a story about the history and nature of the world which we know and inhabit. But it does not tell the full story.

2

The heart's desire

We dream of better worlds – worlds of justice, peace and meaning. The world we see around us often seems to fall short of our aspirations. Somehow, we seem to possess deep intuitions that things shouldn't be like this. William Hazlitt poignantly remarked that man 'is the only animal that is struck with the difference between what things are and what they ought to be'. We observe suffering – and we long for a world in which pain, suffering and death exist no more. We see injustice – and we long for a world in which righteousness will roll down from the mountains like a stream, sweeping away corruption. Surely there must be more to reality than what we see around us! Surely there must be a better world than this!

Maybe these are just consoling thoughts, psychological defences designed to shield us from the harsh realities of life. Then again, they might be clues. They might point to a voice that is calling us, telling us of another land – a land that we once left behind, or a land that we might hope to inhabit in the future. This was certainly the view of J. R. R. Tolkien, whose detailed study of Norse and Anglo-Saxon epics led him to write *The Lord of the Rings*. Tolkien held that the imagination was the key to meaning, opening up worlds that we were meant to see, and in whose light we could understand the enigmas and riddles of life.

In his poem 'Mythopoeia', written in 1931 after a long conversation with C. S. Lewis, Tolkien argues that humanity possesses a homing instinct, an inbuilt sense of our true origins and destiny.[1] The human heart, he wrote, still

> draws some wisdom from the only Wise,
> and still recalls him.

A similar idea is found in the document *Faith and Reason*, issued by Pope John Paul II in 1998. 'God has placed in the human heart a desire to know the truth.' Human beings long to know the truth, and are constantly searching for it – and in doing so, are led home to God, the creator and the ultimate goal of humanity: 'In the far reaches of the human heart there is a seed of desire and nostalgia for God.'[2] Tolkien works with a very similar idea. We dream of enchanted worlds and magic realms, not as a form of escapism, but as a way of discovering and expressing our true identity and destiny.

So how can we make sense of this deep instinct that there is more to life than what we see around us? One obvious answer is to dismiss this intuition as a delusion, a cruel fantasy that we have invented because we cannot cope with the realities of this meaningless world. Although this idea can be found in ancient writers, it was developed by three more recent writers, who each took it in different directions. The German atheist philosopher Ludwig Feuerbach (1804–72) argued that we project our longings and hopes onto some kind of imaginary screen and call this imagined reality 'God'. There is no god, he declares – only a bundle of human hopes and yearnings, which naive humans mistake for God.

Karl Marx (1818–83) developed this idea further. We need to understand why people invent the idea of God in the first place. Marx argued that the cause of this deluded dream of God is social and economic misery: 'Religion is the sigh of the oppressed creature ... It is the opium of the people.' When the socialist revolution came, Marx declared, the cause of belief in God would be removed. Belief in God would wither away. In fact, it did nothing of the sort. The persistence of belief in God in the Soviet Union and its satellite states was a major headache for Marxist theorists. With the collapse of the Soviet Union, religious belief and practice quickly re-established themselves.

Sigmund Freud (1856–1939) argued that belief in God is an illusion, a 'wish-world' resulting from biological and psychological pressures. 'Religious beliefs are illusions, fulfilments of the oldest, strongest and most urgent wishes of humanity.' God is the great sky father, an imaginary source of an equally imaginary protection and comfort. Belief in God is a dream, a wish-fulfilment, which causes psychological damage to people.

Each of these three approaches shares a common theme: the dream of a better world or a loving God is an invention, a human construction which responds to our intellectual, social, or psychological environment. There is no God, nothing transcendent. There is nothing beyond this visible world. Our dreams of another world are simply naive attempts to console ourselves and protect ourselves from the unbearable truth of meaninglessness. Religion is a consoling delusion, the opium of the people.

The Polish poet Czesław Miłosz (1911–2004), who won the Nobel Prize for Literature in 1980, has an interesting point to make about the delusions of modernity. After finding himself stifled intellectually, first under Nazism and then under Stalinism, Czesław had little doubt about the ultimate source of despair and tyranny in the twentieth century. In a remarkable essay titled 'The Discreet Charm of Nihilism', he points out that it is not religion, but its nihilist antithesis, which lies at the root of the century's oppressive totalitarianism:

> Religion, opium for the people! To those suffering pain, humiliation, illness, and serfdom, it promised a reward in afterlife. And now we are witnessing a transformation. A true opium of the people is a belief in nothingness after death – the huge solace of thinking that for our betrayals, greed, cowardice, murders we are not going to be judged.[3]

The Marxist creed has now been inverted. The true opium of modernity is the belief that there is *no* God, so that humans are free to do precisely as they please. We create a moral universe in which we are free to do as we please. There is no ultimate accountability.

These themes have been taken up and developed by many within Western culture, most recently in the New Atheism that developed around 2006, with the publication of Richard Dawkins's *The God Delusion*. The take-home message of this work is simple and direct. Nothing exists outside the natural order, and the most reliable way to understand that order is to apply the scientific method. God is a delusion – an *understandable* delusion, but nonetheless a delusion.

So is belief in God a delusion? C. S. Lewis certainly thought so as a young man, when he was going through an aggressively atheistic phase. Lewis found himself yearning for a world of passion, beauty and meaning which he had come to believe did not and could not exist: 'Nearly all that I loved I believed to be imaginary; nearly all that I believed to be real I thought grim and meaningless.'[4] His imagination told him there was a better world; his reason told him that this was simply nonsense. He therefore believed that he had no option other than to confront the bleakness of a senseless world and his pointless existence. He was forced to choose between an imagined world of beauty and meaning, and an empirical world of futility and hopelessness.

Some will rightly suggest that this represents an unnecessary restriction on possibilities. There might be other ways of making sense of life which accentuate the positives of empirical existence. Yet Richard Dawkins, so diametrically opposed to Lewis on so many issues, would concur with this analysis of the empirical world:

> In a universe of blind physical forces and genetic replication, some people are going to get hurt, other people are going to get lucky, and you won't find any rhyme or reason in it, nor any justice. The universe we observe had precisely the properties we should expect if there is, at bottom, no design, no purpose, no evil and no good, nothing but blind pitiless indifference.[5]

What you see is what you get. There is no evil, no good and no purpose in this blind and meaningless universe. Dawkins would certainly allow that human beings can – and do – *construct* meaning: indeed, one of his basic arguments against religion is that it constructs an arbitrary and delusional belief in order to try to cope with what is fundamentally a meaningless world.[6] For Dawkins, this belief is whimsically imposed upon the world, not legitimately discerned within it. Belief in God is an invention, not an authentic discovery or revelation of reality.

Lewis, however, came to believe that our longing for significance is a marker of something that lies beyond the thresholds of our experience. It is a clue which suggests that human beings are created for something better than the world that we know. For Lewis, human longing is primarily concerned with intimating another transcendent world, the inhabitation of which is the ultimate goal of our life. It is only secondarily concerned with the existence of God, even though this transcendent realm is indeed the 'kingdom of God'. Where Dawkins skims the surface of reality, believing that the superficial appearance of the world is identical with its deep structures, Lewis holds that what we observe is a pointer to something hidden – which, once discovered, changes the way in which we see everything.

Lewis certainly is not alone in having experienced a deep sense of desire for something unknown, possibly unknowable. The English poet Matthew Arnold (1822–88) spoke of German Romantic literature bearing witness to 'a wistful, soft, tearful longing', never fully satisfied by the empirical world. Having experienced intense desire himself, Lewis believed that no theory of reality, no worldview, could be adequate unless it had the capacity to accommodate such experiences. How can such an intense desire, such an inconsolable longing, be accounted for? What purpose does it serve when it seems to be directed towards nothing that we have experienced or can imagine?[7]

The great French philosopher Blaise Pascal (1623–62) saw human longing as a hint pointing towards our true goal:

> What else does this longing and helplessness proclaim, but that there was once in each person a true happiness, of which all that now remains is the empty print and trace? We try to fill this in vain with everything around us, seeking in things that are not there the help we cannot find in those that are there. Yet nobody can change things, because this infinite abyss can only be filled with something that is infinite and unchanging – in other words, by God himself. God alone is our true good.[8]

This is an insight that many have found deeply satisfying. And Lewis came to discover this answer after a long period of atheism, during which he persuaded himself that there was no answer to be found. For many years, Lewis believed that the intense desire that he named 'Joy' was simply a desire for something imaginary. Then he began to realize that it might point towards something that was as real as it was significant. At this point, Lewis's transition concerns not the validity or even the nature of this experience, but its significance. What he had initially thought of as an intense yet ultimately meaningless experience came to be seen in a quite different light. It was seen through a new lens, using a new interpretative framework.

Lewis argues that most people experience a passionate desire for something that simply cannot be had in this world. So how is this to be explained? Lewis explores three main possibilities in his classic work *Mere Christianity*. Some argue that this failure to find satisfaction and delight arises from desiring the wrong things in the world. Once the correct object of human desire is found, true satisfaction will result. And so they commit themselves to a process of restless questing, which never seems to reach or find its goal. Others try to deny and repress the feeling altogether, dismissing it as merely 'wishful thinking' or 'adolescent romanticism'.

Although initially inclined towards the second of these positions, Lewis gradually came to believe that there was a third way of making sense of such a longing: seeing it as a pointer towards another world: 'If I find in myself a desire which no experience in this world can satisfy, the most probable explanation is that I was made for another world.' We are like a skilfully crafted musical instrument, incomplete in the absence of the player, no matter how finely tuned and beautifully constructed. Its potential to create beauty and joy lies unfulfilled.

Yet we must avoid thinking of Christianity simply as a set of ideas or a network of interlocking and interacting concepts. The Christian faith is indeed about a web of ideas, capable of making sense of what we see around us. Yet the Christian vision of reality goes far beyond the limited realm of ideas: it also embraces images, narratives and values. For J. R. R. Tolkien, the central theme is that of 'myth' – a term by which Tolkien really means what we would now term a 'meta-narrative', a story which positions and makes sense of all other stories.[9] A 'myth' is thus not to be understood as something which is untrue, as the everyday use of the word might suggest. For Tolkien, a myth is a narrative of origins, actions and values which gives meaning to events and individuals. It is a vision of reality, refracted through human language and experience.[10]

As illustrated in Tolkien's own writings, such as *The Lord of the Rings*, myths have the power to captivate the human imagination,[11] opening up visions of better and fairer worlds. Tolkien found the notion of a controlling story to be far more powerful and satisfying than a set of ideas. They made a deep appeal to the imagination, offering rich images rather than abstract concepts, descriptions of actions rather than theoretical arguments. Myth, Tolkien came to believe, is essential to human reflection: it governs how we discover our true identity and goal.

Tolkien argued that every culture was founded on an underlying myth: a story that makes sense of history and experience. The modern age is no exception. As Terry Eagleton and other cultural commentators have noted, modernity is based on its own meta-narrative of progress and enlightenment. So how are we to judge these myths, these controlling narratives which set out to make sense of what we see and experience? For Tolkien, the answer lies in the capacity of a myth to explain the enigmas of life. There are many myths, such as the great pagan myths of old and their modern equivalents. Yet each of these myths, he argues, is a reflection or echo of something greater. They are as pieces of glass, refracting a greater light that lies beyond them. All worldviews, whether religious or secular, rest on myths: attempts to account for reality, expressed in many different ways, as splintered fragments of light, each reflecting only some aspects of a greater whole. For Tolkien, Christianity takes the structural form of such a myth. Yet it is the *real* myth, to which all other myths only approximate and aspire. It is the grand narrative, the full picture, which explains and makes sense of other narratives and pictures.

Lewis took a similar view. In a paper entitled 'Is Theology Poetry?' delivered to the Socratic Club at Oxford in 1945, Lewis insists that occasional similarities between Christianity and other religions are to be expected and welcomed, on the basis of the overarching nature of the Christian view of reality. The Christian faith holds that there is some divine illumination vouchsafed to all men. The Divine light, we are told, 'lighteth every man'. We should, therefore, expect to find in the imagination of great Pagan teachers and myth-makers some glimpse of that theme which we believe to be the very plot of the whole cosmic story – the theme of incarnation, death and rebirth.[12]

Lewis argues that Christianity offers a grand narrative which makes sense of all things, which gives rise to sub-narratives that are incomplete, occasionally distorted, refractions of its greater whole. The gospel tells the whole truth, the whole story, setting out a narrative account of reality that allows these sub-narratives to be positioned and explained, while indicating that these only find their completion and fulfilment in that one grand narrative of the Christian gospel, in which 'Myth became Fact'.

It is this gospel meta-narrative, this controlling and illuminating story, Lewis argues, that makes sense of the deep human longing for beauty, significance and meaning. Lewis thus argues that the perennial human 'quest for beauty' is actually a quest for the *source* of that beauty, which is only mediated through the things of this world. It is not contained within them, nor does it ultimately point towards anything in this world. 'The books or the music in which we thought the beauty was located will betray us if we trust to them: it was not *in* them, it only came *through* them, and what came through them was longing.'[13] For Lewis, the desire, the sense of longing, remains with us, 'still wandering and uncertain of its object'. This desire is 'a longing to be reunited with something in the universe from which we now feel cut off, to be on the inside of some door which we have always seen from the outside'.[14]

So where do we truly belong? Where is our homeland? For Lewis, the heart's desire can never be satisfied by anything that is finite or created. A door must be opened so that we can enter into another world, within which our true satisfaction and joy are to be found. *Yet we do not need to leave this world to pass through that door.* As humans, we live in the tension between the world that we know and one that we do not.

Though physically located in one place, we mentally inhabit another, where we believe that we truly belong. 'Paradise is our native land' (Cyprian of Carthage, 200–253). We thus have a homing instinct for another world. Or, to use an image found in the writings of the Renaissance poet Francis Quarles (1592–1644), our soul is like an iron needle drawn to the magnetic pole of God. Though we live here on earth, the beauty, joy and hope of paradise shape our thoughts and actions. The gospel unfolds a story-shaped world which makes sense of the enigmas of our experience – while at the same time offering hope for the future.

Yet our hopes for the future are linked with our understanding of our present situation. As we bring this little book to a conclusion, we may reflect further on how the Christian faith transforms us by opening up new ways of understanding our identity, purpose and value.

3

A transforming vision

The French philosopher Blaise Pascal is one of many to ponder the meaning of life. Is it all a short, meaningless accident?

> When I consider the short duration of my life, swallowed up in the eternity before and after, the little space which I fill, and even which I can see, engulfed in the infinite immensity of spaces of which I know nothing, and which do not know me, I am frightened, and am astonished at being here rather than there. For there is no reason why I am here rather than there, why now rather than then. Who has put me here? By whose order and direction have this place and this time been allotted to me?[1]

Pascal spoke of his fear that his brief occupation of a 'little space' in the vast history of the universe would be random, accidental and devoid of meaning. How could he make sense of things? Reality is open to multiple interpretations. There are different ways of looking at things, with significantly different existential outcomes. Some leave us deeply disturbed, others excite us, some console us. To explore this point, we may consider the night sky. Imagine that you are out on a dark, cold night. Above you, pinpoints of light twinkle in the dark velvet sky. Many have felt overwhelmed by the solemn stillness of the sky at night. But what does it say to us?

It is a question that I have often reflected on myself. When I was nine or ten years old, I managed to build myself a small telescope so I could observe the moons of Jupiter and explore the Milky Way. I spent many a cold winter night staring at the vast expanses of space, wondering where I fitted into all of this. I remember looking at one of the brightest nebulae in the night sky – M31 in Andromeda, now known to be one of the nearest galaxies. Even with my small telescope, I could see something of its beauty. Yet its beauty was tinged with melancholy. I knew that it was more than two million light years away. The light now leaving that distant galaxy would not reach earth for two million years, by which time I would be long since dead. The night sky seemed to me to point to the vastness of the cosmos and the insignificance of humanity.

Much the same thoughts were expressed more recently, though in a much more articulate and reflective manner, by Ursula Goodenough, a cell biologist interested in exploring the deeper meaning of the natural order. She tells of how she became so disturbed by the meaninglessness of the cosmos that she decided to stop thinking about it. 'Our sun too will die, frying the Earth to a crisp during its heat-death, spewing its bits and pieces out into the frigid nothingness of curved spacetime.'[2] She found herself being overwhelmed by a 'bleak emptiness' every time she thought about the deeper meaning of the cosmos. 'The night sky was ruined. I would never be able to look at it again.' In the end, she decided not to think about such things. She decided to cope with the 'the apparent pointlessness of it all' by telling herself that there was no point to seek or to find. As Steven Weinberg once commented, 'The more the universe seems comprehensible, the more it seems pointless.' The information is there – but it doesn't create a pattern. Nothing seems to fit together. There is no big picture.

The classic way of dealing with this troubling realization is Stoic indifference. We should rise above the meaninglessness of the cosmos and concentrate upon building our own character. We create our own problems through our responses to the world. The wise person cultivates a supreme indifference and disengagement from reality, concentrating on the formation of personal character and rationality.[3] Instead of trying to make sense of a senseless universe, the wise person constructs a private rational universe of meaning and value. The development of character is thus an assertion of the individual's capacity to create meaning in the face of a meaningless world. Similar ideas are widely encountered today. Many argue that we must construct our own worlds of meaning, assembling ideas and values into a patchwork quilt of meaning, tailored to our own needs and concerns.

There is, however, an alternative way of looking at things which goes back to the dawn of civilization. Where the New Atheism skims the surface of reality, the wise choose to go deeper. We cannot rest content with a superficial reading of nature. We need to go further and deeper. Meaning, here understood to be embedded deep in the order of things, can be discerned by the wise. It does not need to be constructed or invented; it is already present. The British philosopher and writer Iris Murdoch (1919–99) spoke of 'the calming, whole-making tendencies of human thought', by which she means the ability of a 'big picture' or 'grand narrative' to integrate our vision of reality.

Murdoch is right: we seek meaning in life, rather than endless additional facts about life. It is easy to accumulate information, pasting new items into our mental notebooks in much the same way as a keen stamp collector adds new items to an album. But what purpose does this serve? The poet Edna St Vincent Millay (1892–1950) spoke of 'a meteoric shower of facts' raining from the sky, yet lying on the ground, 'unquestioned, uncombined'. We are overwhelmed with information, as a casual search of the Internet reveals. Yet what bigger picture does this information disclose? What happens when we join together the dots? When we put all the pieces of the jigsaw together? Is there a picture at all? Or is it simply a mass of disconnected bits of information?

Just as the merits of a telescope are judged partly by the clarity with which it allows us to see distant objects, so a worldview is assessed by how well it illuminates the landscape of reality and brings everything into sharp focus. The Christian faith enables us to make sense of things, so that we hear tunes where others only hear noise, and see patterns where others see disorder and chaos. What was once a blurred and fuzzy image is suddenly seen clearly and distinctly.

This is the view that has been explored throughout this little book. The Christian faith offers a framework of meaning which is deeply embedded in the order of things and ultimately originates from and expresses the character of God. The world may indeed seem meaningless and pointless. What is needed, however, is a lens or a conceptual framework which brings things into focus. The world may *seem* meaningless; yet this is because we do not see it in the right way.

C. S. Lewis summed it up well in a well-turned statement: 'I believe in Christianity as I believe that the Sun has risen, not only because I see it, but because by it, I see everything else.'[4]

Yet this framework of meaning is not something that we manage to figure out by ourselves, after an exhaustive analysis of all the options. The meaning that we quest is *disclosed* to us. We are, so to speak, 'surprised by meaning'. The traditional Christian language of 'revelation' affirms that the meaning that all human beings seek, yet find so elusive and mysterious, has been shown to us. Once someone has shown us how to make sense of things, it seems obvious. But we couldn't get there by ourselves. When Thomas H. Huxley first read Darwin's *Origin of Species*, he is reported to have exclaimed: 'How stupid of me not to have thought of that!' Once it had been pointed out to him, it made sense of what Huxley had himself observed. *But Huxley had not been able to find the answer for himself.* Someone had to show him how everything was woven together and interconnected. The Christian faith speaks of a God who holds the key to our history and who has entrusted that key to us so that we might unlock the door to the true meaning of things.

So what kind of meaning are we talking about? The social psychologist Roy Baumeister recently set out a significant analysis of theories of the meaning of life, in which he identified what themes had to be engaged and explored before the human quest for meaning could be satisfied.[5] There were, he argued, four fundamental questions that had to be answered convincingly if a way of thinking was to count as a 'meaning of life':

1 The question of *Identity*: who am I?
2 The question of *Value*: do I matter?
3 The question of *Purpose*: why am I here?
4 The question of *Agency*: can I make a difference?

These are not empirical questions, which can be answered by the natural sciences. As we have seen, they lie beyond its intellectual horizons and methodological frontiers. Yet we cannot live without formulating answers to such questions.

For example, consider the question of justice – a passionate concern for many in today's complex and broken world. Yet justice is not something that we can 'read off' from the world. Indeed, some recent attempts to ground justice in nature sometimes end up defending the Darwinian idea of the 'survival of the fittest'.[6] What of widows and orphans? Of the powerless and weak? In his penetrating and highly acclaimed writings on the nature of justice, Michael J. Sandel argues that any notion of justice depends upon competing conceptions of the good life – that is, networks of beliefs about human nature, values and purpose. Sandel, professor of government at Harvard University, argues that where rationalism held that reason could answer such questions, the harsh reality has turned out to be that they cannot be meaningfully answered without depending upon beliefs that ultimately cannot be proved.[7]

The Enlightenment dream of basing justice on pure reason has foundered. Perhaps more disturbingly for rationalist accounts of reality, such as those favoured by the New Atheism, there is a growing consensus among intellectual historians that the Enlightenment was so diverse that it cannot really be spoken of as a single movement. Instead of speaking of human 'rationality', we must speak of 'rationalities'.[8] The Enlightenment turns out to be a rational multiverse, with competing and diverging accounts of the nature and scope of human reason. That's one of the reasons why so many have concluded that the Enlightenment offered theories of rationality and morality which proved impossible to defend in theory, and impossible to implement in practice.[9] When the New Atheism appeals to reason and morality in defending its own ideas and critiquing those of theists, we are perfectly entitled to ask for clarification. Which rationality do you mean? And which morality?[10]

As Sandel rightly points out, public reason is not neutral: it is shaped by a theory of the good. Secular rationalism therefore does not, and *cannot*, provide an adequate foundation for justice. Sandel argues that secular liberalism represents a hollow and shallow view of the world, which ends up merely defending the right of citizens to do whatever they please, as long as they hurt no one else.[11] But real justice is about values and ideals. Secularism often presents itself as offering a 'neutral' approach to ethics and social questions, allowing all to share in public debate irrespective of their faith commitments. Sandel argues that this is untenable: secularism denies, excludes and suppresses the moral ideals and values of others, while maintaining the myth of its own neutrality.

Sandel's analysis highlights the importance of theories of the meaning of life which bestow value and dignity upon actors and actions. We cannot pretend that there is a 'neutral' public sphere: all spheres of life are shaped by these theories – including the Christian faith. Christianity does more than make sense of things; it also confers meaning and value.

So how does the 'big picture' offered by Christianity engage with these fundamental questions? In what follows, we shall explore each of the four issues we noted earlier in this chapter.

1 Identity: who am I?

It is very easy to give definitions of human identity. We are defined by our genetic make-up, by our social location and by countless other scientific parameters. We can be defined by our race, our nationality, our weight and our gender. Yet all too often, identity is simply reduced to the categories we happen to occupy. The curse of the scientific age is that human beings are reduced to genetic and social stereotypes. Individual identity has become a matter of an impersonal genetic code.

Powerful protests have been raised against this depersonalization of identity. The Jewish philosopher Martin Buber (1878–1965) argued that purely scientific accounts of humanity reduced people to objects: to an 'it' rather than a 'you'. The essence of personal identity, for Buber, is an ability to exist in relationships. We are defined, not by our chemical or genetic make-up, but by our social and personal relationships.[12] Identity is something given, not something achieved. I am given my identity as a father by my children; I am given my identity as a person of significance by the God who has graciously chosen to relate to me and to regard me in this way.

This is a central element of the Christian vision of personal identity and meaning. While the term 'soul' is often misunderstood as an immortal component of human identity, its more biblical meaning is 'human nature in so far as it relates to God'. We find our true identity in our relationship with God, who knows us and gives us our identity and significance. The really important point is this: we do not define ourselves, but we are defined by another, who gives us our identity and significance and safeguards the same. Our identity is not contained in, or safeguarded by, some part of our bodies; it is given and guaranteed by God, who beholds us and remembers us.

Augustine of Hippo made this point in his *Confessions*, written between 397 and 398. Questions of personal identity and significance loom large in this remarkable piece of writing. For Augustine, human destiny and identity are both linked to God, as our creator and redeemer – an idea expressed in Augustine's famous prayer: 'You have made us for yourself, and our heart is restless until it finds its rest in you.'[13] Human identity is here linked with our intentional origination from God and our subsequent relationship with God, culminating in 'finding rest' in God. It is a powerful statement, which suggests a narrative of restoration and homecoming. We are not fully human until we exist in relationship with God. This is a core component of the Christian understanding of human identity.

It's an important point. Many agree that political and social systems ought to enable us to achieve our true humanity. Secular humanism argues that religion suppresses human identity, and it concludes that human liberation is dependent upon the suppression of religion. Yet secular humanism seems to ignore the awkward fact that there are multiple narratives of human identity. Its own theory is simply one among many, and it has no claim to special privilege or priority. Many hold that we only achieve our true identity and fulfilment through relating to God. And that vision of human identity has every right to be heard, represented, and enacted in the public sphere.

2 Value: do I matter?

One of the most profound pieces of writing in the Old Testament is Psalm 8, which takes the form of reflection on the place of humanity in the natural world. The psalmist considers the immensity of the night sky before turning to consider the place of human beings in this vast universe (8.3–5):

> When I look at your heavens, the work of your
>   fingers,
> the moon and the stars that you have established;
> what are human beings that you are mindful of them,
> mortals that you care for them?
> Yet you have made them a little lower than God,
> and crowned them with glory and honour.

The passage locates humanity between God and the beasts of the field, endowed with dignity on account of their divine creation. The fact that God cares for human beings is seen as being a matter for praise rather than logical analysis. The recognition of God's care for individual human beings precedes our reflections on its theological basis. God's care for humanity is emphasized throughout the Old Testament. God is our shepherd, who accompanies, supports and upholds us, even in 'the valley of the shadow of death' (Ps. 23 NIV). Yet the New Testament adds a new dimension to this by reaffirming God's love for humanity by linking to the death of Jesus Christ as a tangible demonstration of this commitment and compassion. Paul speaks of this divine commitment at several points: 'I live by faith in the Son of God, who loved me and gave himself for me' (Gal. 2.20). The death of Christ is not seen primarily as a biological, or even a judiciary, event; it is interpreted as a token of commitment, a demonstration of God's solidarity with humanity.

Our value thus does not depend upon or reflect our achievements; instead, our value comes in the esteem in which we are held by God. God is our 'secure base' (John Bowlby), just as a parent provides the unconditional love and acceptance needed for a child to grow up and learn from mistakes. Such a 'secure base' provides a platform for personal growth and maturation and enables us to cope with personal challenges and difficulties. The biblical image of God or the Christian faith as a 'rock' (as in the image of the person who builds their house on a rock rather than on shifting sand: Matt. 7.24–27) expresses these ideas of security and stability in an accessible way. We possess value because we are valued, accepted and enabled to cope with the challenges of life.

We could speak of the 'transvaluation' of human life through being 'touched' by God – a theme that is found throughout the poetic writings of George Herbert. In one of his poems, Herbert (1593–1633) likens the graceful 'touch' of God to the fabled 'philosopher's stone' of medieval alchemy. Just as the philosopher's stone was believed to transmute base metal into gold, so God could transform the value of individuals through grace:

> This is that famous stone
> That turneth all to gold:
> For that which God doth touch and own
> Cannot for less be told.[14]

We are, as the medieval writer Julian of Norwich famously put it, enfolded in the love of Christ, which brings us a new security, identity and value. Once we see ourselves as enfolded by Christ, we come to think of ourselves in a new way – as those who are valued, welcomed and loved.

3 Purpose: why am I here?

Purpose is central to serious and meaningful living.[15] On the theory of evolution, one of the more disturbing implications of atheistic interpretations is that we are here by accident, the product of an indifferent cosmic happenstance. This conclusion is not, it must be stressed, demanded by evolutionary biology itself; it is the outcome of fusing the basic themes of evolutionary biology with an aggressive and dogmatic atheism. Yet it is an unsettling thought, even for many atheists who profess to believe it. Some, of course, argue that its metaphysical austerity is an indicator of its truth. When I was an atheist myself, I took a certain pride in believing in such grim and bleak ideas, seeing it as a badge of intellectual courage and integrity.

Bleakness, however, is not an indicator of truth. We might believe that everyone is out to get us, so that life is both pointless and downright dangerous. Yet that conclusion might rest upon our somewhat warped interpretation of the world, rather than the reality of the situation. The Christian answer to this question is grounded in the passionate belief that God chose to enter into human history in the life, death and resurrection of Jesus Christ – thus enabling us to relate to God, and ultimately to be with God in the new Jerusalem.

According to Scripture and the Christian tradition, God is the heart's true desire, the goal of our longings, and the fulfiller of our deepest aspirations. The Christian tradition has developed many ways of expressing this belief. The 'chief end' of human existence, according to the Shorter Westminster Catechism (1648), is 'to enjoy God, and glorify him for ever'. God thus provides a rich and deeply satisfying answer to the profound questions that we ask ourselves about the meaning of life.

The image of a journey helps frame the great questions of purpose in life. Some see life as a random and meaning-less process of meandering, in which we search endlessly for a purpose that eludes us, if it exists at all. The Christian tradition sees this journey as having a goal. We walk with a purpose, as we make our way to the new Jerusalem, which is where our true destiny lies. We are, according to the New Testament, 'citizens of heaven', who have the right of abode there. Though in exile on earth, our true homeland lies in heaven. God is our shepherd, the one who leads us, guides us, and accompanies us on our way home.

The journey helps us explore the purpose of life from two different perspectives. First, it emphasizes that life has more than just a direction: moving from life to death. It has a goal, a purpose. To be with God is affirmed to be the culmination of all human desires and longings. Everything that is good, beautiful and true points to God and finds its fulfilment in God. Second, the image of the journey reminds us that we may help others in need along life's road as we travel. Coming home to God and finding rest is the climax of that journey; the process of travelling itself, however, allows us to grow in wisdom and insight and to serve other wayfarers as we travel.

4 Agency: can I make a difference?

Finally, we need to consider an important and often neglected question: can I make a difference? Or am I so insignificant and powerless that I might as well not be here? The capacity to make a difference with things is seen by many people as integral to their quest for meaning and purpose. *If I cannot make a difference, I might as well not be here*, they think. The issue is that of empowerment. Do we have what it takes to make a difference? Or is this something we need to be enabled to do?

From a Christian perspective, human nature is damaged and wounded by sin, thus not able to achieve its full potential unaided. It is a point made throughout the New Testament, particularly in the writings of Paul. As we noted earlier, Paul was convinced that he was trapped, unable to break free from the prison of his own limitations and weaknesses.[16] What could be done? In the end, Paul found his answer: 'Who will rescue me from this body of death? Thanks be to God through Jesus Christ our Lord!' (Rom. 7.24–25).

This theme was particularly developed by Augustine of Hippo, who was exquisitely sensitive to the problem of human weakness, fragility and brokenness.[17] In Augustine's view, human beings were damaged by sin, which was like a hereditary disease, passed down from one generation to another. Sin weakens humanity and cannot be cured by human agency. Yet Christ is the divine physician, by whose 'wounds we are healed' (Isa. 53.5 NIV). We are thus healed by the grace of God, so that our minds may recognize God and our wills may respond to the divine offer of grace.

Or again, Augustine argues that sin is like a power which holds us captive, from whose grip we are unable to break free by ourselves. The human free will is captivated by the power of sin and may only be liberated by grace. Christ is thus seen as the liberator, the source of the grace which breaks the power of sin. Or again, sin is a type of guilt or moral impurity which is passed down from one generation to another. Christ thus comes to bring forgiveness and pardon.

Using such images, Augustine builds up a powerful depiction of human nature being weakened, impoverished and trapped by sin – but healed and liberated by grace.

There is much more that could be said on these themes. The life of faith is to be seen as the divinely enabled pursuit of human aspiration within the recognition of human frailty. It represents an *examined* life, in which each human existence is seen in the mirror of a greater truth and a higher standard. The idea of God's grace gives theological expression to the fundamental Christian experience, hard-wired into the New Testament, that God is one who loves, cares, assists and maintains a faithful watching presence, even in the darkest and loneliest existential moments.

The heart of this life of faith lies not primarily in a set of propositions about reality (although these play an important role), but rather in a trusting orientation and attitude towards God, who is recognized as the sole source of perfection for a being that is clearly intrinsically imperfect. The arrival of God thus brings transformation of our situation, not simply illumination of it.

The all-important point here is that Christianity does not merely enable us to 'make sense of things'. There is a vast chasm between knowledge and meaning, between information and significance. The Christian faith does not leave us where we are, while possessing a better understanding of things; it offers to transform our situation. It may help us to make sense of our situation if we learn that we are ill, or imprisoned. Yet this knowledge of the true state of things is not in itself transformative. Knowing that we are ill does not automatically lead to healing; it is merely the condition for seeking help. But that help lies to hand. As the traditional African American spiritual puts it:

> There is balm in Gilead,
> to make the wounded whole;
> There's power enough in heaven,
> To cure a sin-sick soul.

Conclusion

Recent atheistic writers have ridiculed the idea of 'faith'. Only the deliverances of science and reason are to be trusted! For Richard Dawkins, proprietor of the 'Richard Dawkins Foundation for Reason and Science', faith 'means blind trust, in the absence of evidence, even in the teeth of evidence'.[1] It is a powerful piece of rhetoric, whose influence is matched only by its superficiality.

The truth is obvious, and it is otherwise. Faith is part of the human condition. It is impossible to construct an argument proving the legitimacy of reason without presupposing faith; the conclusion is implicit in the presupposition. As the great feminist philosopher Julia Kristeva put it so trenchantly and clearly: 'Whether I belong to a religion, whether I be agnostic or atheist, when I say "I believe", I mean "I hold as true".'[2]

To hold that something is true and reliable may be *justified* without necessarily being *proved*. I may have good reasons for believing something to be true, yet realize that I cannot prove this is so. That is just the nature of things. Like Charles Darwin, we might believe that we have developed an excellent theory for making sense of what we observe in the world – but not be able to *prove* it, either to ourselves or to others. Like William Wilberforce, we may believe that slavery is unjust and immoral – but not be able to prove that this is so. Happily, this did not stop Wilberforce and others from pursuing justice.

Christianity may be open to criticism on many grounds, but it is certainly not vulnerable to the charge that, in contrast to scientific or empirical thought, it rests on 'mere faith'.[3] We must be critical of our beliefs, subjecting them to interrogation. As Paul insists in one of his earliest letters, 'test everything; hold fast to what is good' (1 Thess. 5.21). Where Dawkins thinks Christians believe blindly, the New Testament holds them to believe reliably and critically, on the basis of the evidence available.

In this little book, we have explored the deep human desire to make sense of things, evident in both the natural sciences and in the Christian faith. We often seem to have a sense of standing on the brink of something greater, lying beyond the horizons of experience and reason. What we do know seems to point beyond itself, to a greater vision of reality. Voices seem to call to us from the ends of the earth, pointing to something deeper and better than anything we presently possess or know. As the poet Matthew Arnold (1822–88) puts it in 'The Buried Life':

> But often, in the world's most crowded streets,
> But often, in the din of strife,
> There rises an unspeakable desire
> After the knowledge of our buried life.

Our engagement with the world awakens a deeper sense of longing, which goes beyond simply making sense of things. We want to be part of something deeper, to be able to be part of a bigger picture. The Christian way of seeing things makes cognitive and existential sense of reality, offering us a powerful, persuasive and attractive account of ourselves, our universe and why we are here.

Christianity does not simply make sense *to* us; it also makes sense *of* us. It positions us in the great narrative of cosmic history and locates us on a mental map of meaning. It offers us another way of seeing things, offers us another way of living, and invites us to share these. We need a frame of reference, which offers us a secure foundation and focus for our lives.

For Christians, this foundation and focus is the living God, the 'God and Father of our Lord Jesus Christ' (2 Cor. 1.3). This God makes himself known in the life, death and resurrection of Jesus Christ, and in the pages of Scripture. But he also makes something of himself known through the natural world, the world of creation, as a voice which calls us, beckoning from its depths and mysterious beauty.

For things of this world are but signs and pointers; and if we really want to understand why we are here we must let them lead us to their source.

Notes

1 Beyond the scientific horizon

1 Thomas H. Huxley, *Darwiniana* (London: Macmillan, 1893), 248–52, with quote from 252.

2 See Thomas H. Huxley, *Collected Essays*, vol. 4 (London: Macmillan, 1895), 139–63.

3 Charles Darwin, *The Life and Letters of Charles Darwin*, ed. Francis Darwin, 3rd edn, 3 vols. (London: John Murray, 1887), 2:200.

4 For what follows, see José Ortega y Gasset, *History as a System and Other Essays toward a Philosophy of History* (New York: W. W. Norton, 1962), 13–15.

5 Charles A. Coulson, *Science and Christian Belief* (Chapel Hill, NC: University of North Carolina Press, 1958), 75.

6 Richard Swinburne, *The Existence of God* (Oxford: Clarendon Press, 1979), 71.

7 On this further, see John Polkinghorne, *One World: The interaction of science and theology* (Princeton, NJ: Princeton University Press, 1986).

8 Albert Einstein, 'Physics and Reality', *Journal of the Franklin Institute* 221 (1936): 349–89, with quote from 351.

9 Stephen Jay Gould, 'Impeaching a Self-Appointed Judge', *Scientific American* 267, no. 1 (1992): 118–21.

10 M. R. Bennett and P. M. S. Hacker, *Philosophical Foundations of Neuroscience* (Oxford: Blackwell, 2003), 372–76.

2 The heart's desire

1 J. R. R. Tolkien, *Tree and Leaf* (London: HarperCollins, 2001), 87. For the idea in Reformed theology, see Charles

Hodge, *Systematic Theology,* 3 vols. (New York: Scribner's, 1917), 1:200. Hodge here argues that God is the true goal of 'our religious feelings, our sense of dependence, our consciousness of responsibility [and] our aspirations after fellowship with some Being higher than ourselves, and higher than anything which the world or nature contain'.

2 John Paul II, encyclical letter *Fides et Ratio,* 24. Text at http://www.vatican.va/holy_father/john_paul_ii/encyclicals/documents/hf_jp-ii_enc_15101998_fidesetratio_en.html.

3 Czesław Miłosz, 'The Discreet Charm of Nihilism', *New York Times Review of Books,* 19 November 1998, 17–18. For his best and most influential book, see Czesław Miłosz, *The Captive Mind* (New York: Vintage Books, 1981).

4 C. S. Lewis, *Surprised by Joy* (London: Collins, 1989), 138.

5 Richard Dawkins, *River out of Eden: A Darwinian view of life* (London: Phoenix, 1995), 133.

6 For an assessment of Dawkins's arguments at this point, see Keith Ward, *Why There Almost Certainly Is a God: Doubting Dawkins* (Oxford: Lion Hudson, 2008).

7 For a full discussion, see John Haldane, 'Philosophy, the Restless Heart, and the Meaning of Theism', *Ratio* 19 (2006): 421–40.

8 Blaise Pascal, *Pensées* (New York: Penguin, 1995), 45.

9 Here see Verlyn Flieger, *Splintered Light: Logos and language in Tolkien's world* (Kent, OH: Kent State University Press, 2002), 9–10.

10 Christopher Garbowski, *Recovery and Transcendence for the Contemporary Mythmaker: The spiritual dimension in the works of J. R. R. Tolkien* (Lublin, Poland: Marie Curie-Skłodowska University Press, 2000).

11 Jane Chance, *The Lord of the Rings: The mythology of power* (Lexington, KY: University Press of Kentucky, 2001).

12 C. S. Lewis, 'Is Theology Poetry?' in *C. S. Lewis: Essay collection and other short pieces,* ed. Lesley Walmsley (London: HarperCollins, 2000), 1–21, with quote from 15–16.

13 C. S. Lewis, 'The Weight of Glory', in *Screwtape Proposes a Toast, and Other Pieces* (London: Collins Fontana Books, 1965), 98–99.

14 Ibid., 106.

3 A transforming vision

1 Blaise Pascal, *Pensées* (New York: Penguin, 1995), 19.

2 Ursula Goodenough, *The Sacred Depths of Nature* (Oxford: Oxford University Press, 1998), 10.

3 See further Richard Sorabji, *Emotion and Peace of Mind: From Stoic agitation to Christian temptation* (Oxford: Oxford University Press, 2002), 17–54.

4 C. S. Lewis, 'Is Theology Poetry?' in *C. S. Lewis: Essay collection and other short pieces*, ed. Lesley Walmsley (London: HarperCollins, 2000), 1–21, with quote from 21.

5 Roy Baumeister, *Meanings of Life* (New York: Guilford Press, 1991), 29–57.

6 As noted and documented by Richard Weikart, *From Darwin to Hitler: Evolutionary ethics, eugenics, and racism in Germany* (New York: Palgrave Macmillan, 2004).

7 Michael J. Sandel, *Justice: What's the right thing to do?* (New York: Farrar, Straus & Giroux, 2009), 244–69.

8 See, for example, James Schmidt, *What Is Enlightenment? Eighteenth-century answers and twentieth-century questions* (Berkeley, CA: University of California Press, 1996).

9 See the analysis in Robert J. Louden, *The World We Want: How and why the ideals of the Enlightenment still elude us* (Oxford: Oxford University Press, 2007).

10 See the classic analysis in Alasdair MacIntyre, *Whose Justice? Which Rationality?* (Notre Dame, IN: University of Notre Dame Press, 1988).

11 Michael J. Sandel, *Liberalism and the Limits of Justice* (Cambridge: Cambridge University Press, 1982).

12 Maurice S. Friedman, *Martin Buber: The life of dialogue*, 4th edn (London: Routledge, 2002).

13 Augustine of Hippo, *Confessions* 1.1.1.

14 For a detailed theological commentary on Herbert's *Elixir*, from which this stanza is taken, see Alister McGrath,

'The Gospel and the Transformation of Reality: George Herbert's "Elixir"', in *The Passionate Intellect: Christian faith and the discipleship of the mind* (Downers Grove, IL: InterVarsity Press, 2010), 45–55.

15 For a classic account of this point, see Rick Warren, *The Purpose-Driven Life: What on earth am I here for?* (Grand Rapids, MI: Zondervan, 2002).

16 Paul writes, e.g., 'I can will what is right, but I cannot do it. For I do not do the good I want, but the evil I do not want is what I do' (Rom. 7.18–19).

17 See Alister McGrath, *Heresy: A history of defending the truth* (San Francisco: HarperOne, 2009), 159–70.

Conclusion

1 Richard Dawkins, *The Selfish Gene*, 2nd ed. (Oxford: Oxford University Press, 1989), 198.

2 Julia Kristeva, *The Incredible Need to Believe* (New York: Columbia University Press, 2009), 3.

3 For an excellent engagement with this point, see Timothy Keller, *The Reason for God: Belief in an age of skepticism* (New York: Dutton, 2008), 127–225.

Further reading

Here is a short list of books that can guide you further in your exploration of the topics discussed in this book.

The text of *Why Are We Here?* is drawn from chapters 6, 12 and 13 of the author's *Surprised by Meaning: Science, faith and how we make sense of things* (WJK, 2011).

Alister McGrath, *Inventing the Universe: Why we can't stop talking about science, faith and God* (Hodder & Stoughton, 2015)

Jonathan Sacks, *The Great Partnership: God, science and the search for meaning* (Hodder & Stoughton, 2011)

Other books of related interest (all published by SPCK):
Alister McGrath, *The Dawkins Delusion?* (2007)
Alister McGrath, *Why God Won't Go Away* (2011)
Alister McGrath, *The Living God* (2013)
John Polkinghorne, *Quarks, Chaos and Christianity* (2005)
John Polkinghorne, *Science and Religion in Quest of Truth* (2011)
Gillian Straine, *Introducing Science and Religion: A path through polemic* (2013)